Original title:
Searching for the Meaning of Life… Call Me When You Find It

Copyright © 2025 Creative Arts Management OÜ
All rights reserved.

Author: Cameron Blair
ISBN HARDBACK: 978-1-80566-053-8
ISBN PAPERBACK: 978-1-80566-348-5

The Unraveled Fabric of Clarity

In a world of questions, I roam free,
Like a bee who forgot where the flowers be.
Wandering through thoughts, lost in my head,
Searching for wisdom where logic has fled.

I asked my cat, he just stared me down,
He rolled on his back, then he twirled around.
Maybe the answer's under the rug,
Or hiding in soup, like an old, warm mug.

I tried talking to clouds up in the sky,
But they laughed at my jokes, and just floated by.
Perhaps life's a riddle wrapped in a joke,
Or a pickle jar waiting for someone to poke.

One day I'll trip on the path of delight,
And stumble upon wisdom while taking a bite.
Until then, I'll swirl in this amusing ballet,
Chasing my thoughts like a dog with a fray.

Answers Blowing in the Wind

Caught in a breeze, my thoughts take flight,
Like a squirrel with acorns in a wobbly sight.
I chase after whispers that dance through the air,
But they giggle and tease, not a care in their flair.

I once found a fortune cookie's crack,
It said, 'Life's a mystery, don't look back.'
So I took its advice and fell in a hole,
Where I laughed with shadows, and danced with a mole.

The trees have their secrets, but they won't spill,
They'd rather play games, like hide and seek thrill.
Maybe the answer's stuck in the grass,
Waiting for someone with time to amass.

Wandering on paths that lead to nowhere,
I hope for a sign, or at least a good share.
As I search for solutions, through giggles and spins,
I'll toast with the stars and see where it begins.

Constellations of Uncertainty

Stars in my coffee, they swirl and they spin,
Sometimes they dance, and sometimes they grin.
Questions like comets shoot through the night,
Mapping my thoughts with twinkling delight.

Asteroids fall with a crash and a boom,
I ponder my purpose while cleaning my room.
Planets align with my breakfast delights,
Finding my way through the cosmic fright.

The Journey Beyond the Known

Hopped on a bus with a map made of cheese,
Drivers of fate laugh as they tease.
Stops along the way, each one a surprise,
Filled with odd folks and their glittery lies.

A clown in the corner is juggling my doubts,
While penguins in suits barter eccentric routes.
Every turn brings a joke or a dance,
I trip on my thoughts, but hey, what's the chance?

Reflections in the Mirror of Existence

I gaze at myself, what do I behold?
A patchwork of dreams filled with laughter so bold.
The mirror just chuckles and says, 'What's the fuss?'
'Your life's a great show, hop back on the bus!'

Makeup of memories paint my face with a grin,
While shadows of self-doubt peel off like old skin.
Each wrinkle a tale, each smile a prank,
Here's to my story, however you rank!

Notes from an Infinite Road

On the highway of humor, I drive with a song,
Wheels made of laughter, the journey feels long.
GPS lost but my spirits are high,
I fuel up on giggles, I'll never say die.

Road signs remind me to slow down and see,
Life's quirky moments, like ants having tea.
I wave to the cows as they moo out a tune,
In this circus of life, I'm a dancing cartoon!

The Dance of Unasked Questions

Why do socks always disappear,
Yet always have a partner, dear?
Is the universe just playing games,
Hiring clowns with silly names?

Do fish ever get thirsty, too?
Or is their swim a drink for you?
What's the secret behind a sneeze?
Maybe it's just the wind's tease!

Why do we dream of flying high,
When waking makes us say goodbye?
Is twilight really the day's last laugh,
Or a cat with a secret path?

Questions twirl in funny ways,
Like a waltz through foggy days.
We'll dance till dawn without a clue,
Hoping answers come into view.

Ripples in the Water of Now

Gazing at the pond's reflection,
Wondering about my own direction.
Do frogs think they'll leap forever,
Or just hop to avoid the endeavor?

The sun winks at clouds drifting by,
Are they plotting a little spy?
Is rain just nature's way to play,
Or a gentle reminder it's laundry day?

Fish flip and flop in delight,
Do they dream of a cozy night?
Or swirl in circles for sheer fun,
While poets ponder what they've done?

Ripples form and fade away,
Like thoughts that go astray.
I'm here, with laughter on my brow,
Seeking answers, wondering how.

The Hunt for Hidden Clarity

With a magnifying glass in hand,
I search for sense in this vast land.
Is cereal's crunch a breakfast thrill,
Or a way to top off a milk-filled hill?

The map to wisdom's curled and worn,
Do you find clarity where it's torn?
If life's a puzzle missing a piece,
Must I compete or find my peace?

Kittens seem wise beyond their years,
While sipping milk, they conquer fears.
Is a nap the answer we've sought,
Or just a clever plot by the cat squad?

Each clue I gather, turns to jest,
Life's riddle feels like a spirited quest.
With laughs and hiccups, I stride forth,
Hoping for clarity's grand rebirth.

Layers of Dust on Ancient Scrolls

In a dusty library of old tales,
Are scholars' thoughts wrapped in veils?
Could wisdom be hiding, taking a bath,
Or just unsure of its own path?

Each scroll whispers secrets untold,
But my patience is growing cold.
Do the ancients chuckle in their slumber,
While I'm left with crumpled wonder?

I sneeze and send the dust a-flying,
As echoes of laughter go sprawling.
Did they know the end was a golden prize,
Or just a clever way to disguise?

Layers build like cakes of lore,
Teasing, but always wanting more.
So let's unwrap with a giggle or two,
And see what old minds hid from view.

Threads of Existence

Tangled in a web, I roam,
Chasing thoughts not close to home.
A sock, a shoe, where's my guide?
Life's a ride, let's laugh and slide.

Puppies chase their tails for fun,
I chase my dreams, but where's the sun?
Every corner holds a riddle,
Life's a tune, I play the fiddle.

Jokes on me when plans go awry,
Like losing keys, oh me, oh my!
But with each trip, a tale I'll weave,
In foolish thoughts, I still believe.

Each moment feels like quite the scene,
Like carrots wearing hats, so keen.
With every laugh, I play my part,
In this circus called life, with a happy heart.

The Muse of Wandering Souls

A compass broken, oh what luck,
Lost in thoughts, I'm just a schmuck.
My shoes are worn, my map's a joke,
Yet I wander like a happy bloke.

With every twist of fate, I grin,
Like rubber bands that stretch within.
I search for wisdom in the sky,
While squirrels mock me, oh my, oh my!

My GPS is just a friend,
It leads me on a laugh-filled trend.
In the wild, I might just stay,
With nature's puns to save the day.

So here's to journeys, big and small,
With hiccups lingering, I'll stand tall.
If meaning hides like missing socks,
I'll dance the jig and laugh with cocks.

Navigation Through the Dark

With a flashlight on my chin, I tread,
Looking for sense in every bed.
Why'd I come here? Who can tell?
Maybe life's a joke, oh well!

In murky nights, I seek the light,
Bumping into walls, oh what a sight.
Laughter echoes in the night,
As shadows play tricks, giving fright.

A map of stars spins overhead,
While pizza cravings fill my head.
Every detour's just a game,
As I stumble, still feeling fame.

What's the goal? Oh, who could know?
Maybe it's just to steal the show.
In darkened alleys, wisdom hides,
With giggles trailing, as hope guides.

A Wanderer's Epistemology

Philosophers sit with frowns so deep,
While I trip over, losing sleep.
What's this all about, they say with haste,
While I'm busy planning my next feast.

With every step, I ponder more,
Like socks that vanish, what's in store?
In deck chairs of life, I lounge and stare,
While universes wink, quite debonair.

Every question leads to more of me,
Like floating thoughts on a busy sea.
In absurdity, truth ebbs and flows,
While laughter's the path that always glows.

So here I am, a fool in hand,
With breadcrumbs scattered through this land.
Seek wisdom? Sure, if it's a snack,
But first, let's find that wayward sock back.

The Pulse of Untamed Wonder

In a world so vast and wide,
I chase the squirrel, filled with pride.
The breadcrumbs lead to nowhere fast,
Yet my laughter echoes, unsurpassed.

With morning coffee, dreams collide,
A donut hole, my trusted guide.
I glance at clouds that dance in jest,
Each shape I see, I must invest.

With tickling thoughts and goofy grins,
I ponder where the journey begins.
A wild goose chase or simply fun,
Each silly step, I'm never done.

So here I tread, with joy unbound,
In laughter's arms, I'm surely found.
The pulse of wonder checks my pace,
Life's a riddle, full of grace.

Temporal Question Marks

A clock ticks loud, or is that me?
Dancing with shadows, oh so free.
Time's a trickster, spinning round,
In laughter's court, I've been crowned.

Why do socks vanish, who can say?
They slip and slide, oh what a play!
With every tick, I shrug and grin,
As I chase my dog, that silly twin.

Lost in moments of pure delight,
I juggle cupcakes, what a sight!
Each question mark is like a clown,
In temporal loops, I'm turning 'round.

So let's embrace the whimsy here,
With laughter's song, we have no fear.
In seconds' laughter, life's a spark,
A dance of joy, a bright hallmark.

Resonance in a Sea of Stillness

In a quiet room, my thoughts take flight,
With socks mismatched, I feign insight.
A catwalk strut on wobbly chairs,
A serenade to life's odd pairs.

In stillness echoes, humor glows,
I ponder why the garden grows;
The weeds jump up, they claim their space,
Yet I still dance, a silly grace.

With every question that I scribble,
I find a joke; my heart will giggle.
The stillness reigns, yet here I stand,
Laughing softly, life unplanned.

So here's to all the questions posed,
In silent fun, life's truth is close.
The sea of stillness, waves of cheer,
In laughter's tide, I steer clear.

Searchlights on the Journey

With searchlights bright, I roam the night,
In hot pursuit of a lost delight.
The moon plays tricks, a glimmering tease,
As I trample through the tall, wild trees.

I glance below, the shadows leap,
What secrets hide where I must creep?
The critters giggle, oh, what a sight,
In this wild hunt, it feels so right.

With every stumble, I find a clue,
A rubber chicken, what's that to you?
Each step I take, the laughter grows,
In absurdity, the journey flows.

So light the way with laughter's spark,
Embrace the joy, don't miss the mark.
With searchlights on, I play the part,
In silly quests, I find my heart.

Echoes of Infinite Quest

In the land of lost socks, I roam,
Chasing dreams that dance like foam.
A llama in a suit offers tea,
But what does it all mean to me?

With a map made of spaghetti,
And riddle-phrases all quite petty.
I ask the gnome with a top hat near,
For wisdom with a splash of beer.

I follow the breadcrumbs of my fate,
Yet end up debating a giant plate.
When will I find that elusive rhyme,
Or is this just a waste of time?

The universe laughs, a cosmic jest,
As I embark on another quest.
Juggling questions, both big and small,
I'll find the answer, or not at all.

The Night Whispers Unanswered

Under the stars that wink and tease,
I ponder questions over cheese.
A talking cat with a monocle sighs,
Life's puzzles hidden behind its eyes.

I ride a broomstick made of brie,
As constellations joke about me.
Each twinkle hints at truths unsaid,
While squirrels debate what lies ahead.

In moonlit kitchens, pots clatter loud,
Chasing wisdom in a pancake cloud.
Thoughts flip like pancakes over the stove,
But do they hold the answers I love?

As shadows dance in the silent night,
I laugh at the vastness of my plight.
When will the universe drop a clue,
Or is the punchline always on cue?

Footprints on the Edge of Understanding

I walked on clouds made from soft fluff,
Cursing the day when things get tough.
Footprints of wisdom muddled in mud,
How to decipher the cosmic thud?

A refrigerator hums a secret tune,
While chairs gossip about the moon.
Do flowers chat with the buzzing bees?
Or is that just my mind, trying to please?

Each step, a question, a path uncharted,
With my trusty sock puppet, we've started.
Is there an answer beneath this shoe?
Or just a reminder to laugh with you?

Each footprint fades like a whispered song,
With each new question, I still tag along.
Echoes of answers and laughter in time,
Maybe the point is the fun of the climb.

Beneath the Veil of Existence

In a world where jellybeans reign supreme,
I ponder life's weird little dream.
Do clouds hold secrets or just rain?
While waiters drop clues with a side of pain.

A toaster speaks of golden toast,
While I search for meaning, it's what I need most.
Do fish find wisdom in their watery run?
Or are they just swimming, having some fun?

Under the veil of a pancake sky,
I wonder if frogs ever question why.
Do they leap for answers or just for play?
With no response—guess I'll frolic away.

Life's a circus, and I'm the clown,
In a world that spins round and round.
Maybe the answer's tucked deep inside,
Or just a punchline to giggle and ride.

Lighthouses in the Fog

In a sea of socks, I drift away,
Chasing thoughts that lead astray.
Dancing shadows, lost and bold,
Here's my compass, but it's sold.

Bumbling through life, a sneaky dance,
Hoping someday to find my chance.
Yet every twist, a laugh in tow,
Life's a sitcom with no show.

We've got maps that lead to snacks,
And guidebooks filled with silly facts.
So here I stand, one foot in dream,
Life's a carnival—come join the theme!

With clowns and hats of every hue,
I search for meaning, just like you.
But hold the popcorn; life's a joke,
We're all just punchlines, make no mistake!

The Heart's Unending Scroll

My heart's a scroll, with doodles thick,
Of dreams and laughs, and clever tricks.
I turn the pages, winking wide,
For wisdom lost, I cannot hide.

Serendipity strikes, like a cat with grace,
As I trip on fate, a funny face.
Chasing truth in wigs and fun,
Juggling purpose, one by one.

Yet down the line, a hot dog stand,
Makes me ponder where I stand.
Perhaps life's secret's ketchup brown,
Or mustard yellow, all around!

So here I scribble, with pen in fist,
Searching for meaning, as if I've missed.
In laughter's echo, I take my role,
As the jester, with an empty scroll.

An Exploration of the Invisible

In the corner, dust bunnies meet,
They've got stories, none can beat.
I reach for magic, but all I find,
Is my cat staring, utterly blind.

I chase the whispers of yesterday,
But they giggle and just run away.
Invisible answers, floating around,
Like confetti lost, can't be found.

So here I am, a curious sprite,
With a flashlight, seeking a bite.
Life's a riddle, dressed in fog,
I'm lost at sea, on a leapfrog bog!

Yet every ghost has a hearty cheer,
When I ask them, "Can you steer?"
They just chuckle and float on by,
Oh life, you sly little pie!

The Quest for Effervescent Truth

With bubbles popping, I try to think,
Does truth come in a drink?
Each sip a riddle, oh so bright,
Yet more like soda; where's the insight?

I quest for wisdom in every fizz,
Seeking answers—wait, what is this?
A pineapple slice floats by my cup,
Stirring the chaos, I'll drink it up!

Wrapped in tinsel, my brain goes pop,
As I ponder the human hop.
Hopscotch games of fate and flair,
Bubble wrap thoughts, floating in air.

So join my quest for filters fun,
As I chase a truth on the run.
With laughter ringing in each clink,
Life's a party—so let's not think!

When Questions Outnumber Stars

Why is the sky so very high?
Do fish ever dream of flying?
Why do ducks waddle, oh so spry?
And where do socks go when they're crying?

Is the moon a giant cheese wheel?
Does laughter have a taste or feel?
Why do we chase what we can't steal?
And why's the clock always on a squeal?

Can the trees hear the gossip in the wind?
Why do we ask things that have no end?
Is the sun the world's hottest friend?
Why do we pretend to comprehend?

In a world of questions bright and vast,
Will we find answers, or just have a blast?
As we laugh at the moments that fade so fast,
Let's revel in riddles, let joy be our cast.

Emptiness Adorned with Wonder

What fills the void of my missing sock?
Is it a creature that likes to mock?
Does it dance with glee as I tick-tock?
Or does it just sit—waiting to unlock?

Why do we chase the last cookie jar?
Is it a prize or a battle scar?
Can crumbs hold secrets from near or far?
Or just announce we've gone too bizarre?

Do animals giggle when we wear shoes?
What fortune lies hidden in our snooze?
Must we always ponder and keep our dues?
What if the answers are all just blues?

Amidst the silence where laughs should gleam,
Is there a grand plan, or just a dream?
Wrapped in riddles like a cozy seam,
Finding joy, whatever the theme.

The Light Behind Closed Doors

What lurks behind that old, creaky door?
Is it secrets, or socks I adore?
Perhaps a dance party with a dinosaur?
Or maybe a vacuum, tired and sore?

Do we hear echoes of wisdom or jest?
What foolish thoughts clutter our quest?
Is that light a beacon, or just a fest?
Or merely the fridge we don't want to test?

Why do we keep searching for shiny gold?
Is it warmth, laughter, or tales to be told?
What's in the quiet? A mystery bold?
Or just the cat dreaming of fish—so cold?

Behind each door, a new world may peak,
With giggles and grumbles and laughter to speak.
Who knows what wonders the shadows will leak?
Maybe just tales from the fridge, quite unique.

A Tapestry of Yearning Questions

Why do we crowd the mirrors in lines?
Are we looking for truth or shiny designs?
Is the heart a puzzle that never aligns?
Or just a place where pure chaos shines?

Does the sun still whisper secrets to moles?
Do clouds hold stories in curlicue rolls?
What do butterflies think as they stroll?
Is it freedom packed tight in their souls?

Is wisdom a hunt for a very lost key?
Or a donut spinning just for the glee?
Can warmth be found in a joke or decree?
Or is it all nonsense you'll never foresee?

In this vibrant web where whims run wild,
Are we kids at heart, delightfully riled?
Chasing the giggles, feeling beguiled,
Lost in the wonder, forever beguiled.

Chasing the Elusive Answer

I asked a wise man for his thought,
He scratched his head as if he'd fought.
His beard was long, his shoes were old,
But answers seem a bit too bold.

I paraded round the coffee shop,
With questions that would never stop.
The barista laughed, she rolled her eyes,
"Dude, just sip your latte, don't be shy!"

Through every book, I flipped that page,
Each riddle seemed to fuel my rage.
The last word found was "abracadabra,"
Now all that's left is empty cabbages.

So here I am, on this wild spree,
I'll search for my truth in a cup of tea.
Perhaps tomorrow, or after lunch,
I'll find that wisdom, or just a crunch.

The Heart's Compass

With a map that's drawn in crayon hues,
I'm lost in thought, with whimsical views.
My heart's a compass that spins and twirls,
It points to cake and twinkling pearls.

I asked a cat where I should roam,
She merely yawned, and found a home.
A squirrel ran past with a peanut stash,
He shouted, "Life's a crazy bash!"

So I followed birds with joking songs,
They chirped of love and righting wrongs.
But when I asked them where to go,
They flew away, oh the show!

"Your heart knows best!" a mouse did squeak,
I pondered hard, yet felt so weak.
But between the cheese and midnight snacks,
I'll find my way—no looking back!

Vagabond Thoughts in the Wilderness

In a forest deep, I wandered free,
With thoughts dancing like leaves on a spree.
I tripped on roots, a faceplant delight,
One tree chuckled, "You're quite the sight!"

A raccoon peeked from behind a trunk,
He sold me dreams with a hint of funk.
"Life's like a taco, messy and bold,
Just add some salsa; watch how it unfolds!"

I scribbled notes on a fallen leaf,
Jokes about joy and just a bit of grief.
Each vine had secrets I longed to know,
But all I found was a funky show.

So here in the woods, I'll laugh and muse,
With critters as friends and nothing to lose.
In this wild page, I'll write my own tale,
With giggles and grins that never pale.

Searching for the Light Within

I searched my room for signs of grace,
Only found socks and a cereal trace.
In the mirror, my hair was wild,
Is this the light? I'd still be a child!

With candles lit for added flair,
I thought I'd find enlightenment there.
Instead, a cat jumped in the flame,
She purred and claimed she had no shame.

A flashlight broke during this quest,
The bulb went pop—oh, what a jest!
I danced with shadows, made my own vibe,
Who knew the dark could be so tribe?

So if you're lost, don't fret or pine,
Sometimes the silly is the grand design.
I'll laugh with the stars, shine just as bright,
And maybe find my spark tonight!

Embracing the Unseen

I wander through the quirks of fate,
With questions piled up like a messy plate.
From socks to stars, I ponder with glee,
As if wisdom hides behind the next cup of tea.

Why did the chicken cross the light?
To chase a dream, or avoid a bite?
Each riddle brings laughter, a chuckle or two,
Yet no answers are coming, not even a clue.

The universe laughs, oh what a tease,
It flicks me a wink, like a playful breeze.
I'm stumbling along, on this comedic spree,
Perhaps the joke's really on me!

So here's to the search, with a smile so wide,
Through the unexplained, let humor be my guide.
In moments of wonder, I'll lift up my voice,
For laughter, it seems, was always my choice.

A Symphony of Unanswered Whispers

Notes of confusion dance in my head,
For answers are packed away, kept in a shed.
A symphony plays with a wild, bouncy tune,
While I'm stuck rehearsing beneath the silvery moon.

The universe hums, its secrets untold,
Like a magician who never grows old.
I wave my wand, but tricks just don't show,
Maybe the punchline is part of the flow.

I laugh at the questions that swirl in my mind,
Like socks in a dryer, they weave and unwind.
Each twist is a giggle, a tickle, a tease,
Why think too hard? I'll just dance with ease.

So if you hear whispers, just take a seat,
With a wink and a nod, isn't life a treat?
In this wacky parade of curious sights,
I'll clap to the rhythm of puzzling delights!

Threads of Fate and Understanding

Life's tapestry's woven in colors bizarre,
I tug at the threads, search each shining star.
With every pull, a new laugh unfolds,
But clear understanding? That query's on hold.

Like a jester in court, I prance and I play,
In this grand game of life, come what may.
I juggle my thoughts, they slip and they slide,
Oh, where's the manual? I wish I could hide.

Each knot is a giggle, each fray a delight,
In a world that spins like a top in the night.
I'm weaving my way through this humorous maze,
As patience and wit set my heart all ablaze.

So here's to the threads, so glorious and bright,
In the quest for the answers, let laughter ignite.
With a flourish and bow, I embrace the unknown,
For perhaps this riddle's the best kind of throne!

The Horizon of Yearning

I stand at the edge, with a grin on my face,
Peering ahead at this curious place.
The horizon awaits, with riddles in tow,
Like a pizza joke, it's the punchline I sow.

Clouds may be feisty, the stars might confuse,
But tripping on dreams, I'm never to lose.
With laughter as ballast, I sail through the night,
I'll giggle at shadows that dance in the light.

The view is spectacular, oh what a sight,
Fumbling for meaning with all of my might.
But maybe, just maybe, the fun is the goal,
And the search is the journey that tickles my soul.

So raise up a toast to the horizon I chase,
For in the absurdity, I find my own space.
With a wink to the cosmos, I'll stride without fear,
For it's laughter that makes all the answers seem near!

The Quest That Never Ends

With maps drawn in crayon, I roam the night,
Chasing shadows and giggles, oh what a sight.
My compass spins wildly, it just can't decide,
To find treasures of wisdom or just popular tide.

Each step feels like dancing on a jellybean,
I ponder the questions no one's ever seen.
Is it here in the cookie, or perhaps in a wink?
If only my plans didn't fizzle and sink.

Walking the Tightrope of Tomorrow.

Balancing dreams on a wire so thin,
Wobbling through wonders where giggles begin.
The crowd is all cheering, but what do they know?
Do they see my great stumble, or just my wild show?

With each little misstep, laughter will bloom,
I'm flinging my thoughts to the stars, then the gloom.
Tomorrow's a puzzle, wrapped in a bow,
That tickles your fancy and steals the last show.

Echoes of the Uncharted Path

On roads paved with marshmallows, I twirl with glee,
Though they stick to my shoes like life's mystery.
The echoes are chuckling, I follow the sound,
For wisdom's a riddle so goofy and round.

I dip my toes in puddles, bright as a dream,
In this wacky adventure, nothing's as it seems.
Each twist is a giggle, each turn a surprise,
With a wink and a nudge, I embrace the wise lies.

Whispers in the Void

In the silence of night, I hear silly calls,
It's the universe laughing as mystery falls.
The void sings a tune that's both sweet and absurd,
In the quest for life's answers, no one's truly heard.

I put on my shades, ready for the ride,
With a wink at the void and my secrets to hide.
Oh, what a strange game this circus we play,
Always seeking the meaning, as it drifts far away.

Light Beneath the Tides

In a world of wobbly signs,
I chase goldfish in the brines.
Saltwater tickles my bare feet,
While I ponder life's grand treat.

Nudging crabs with playful glee,
Wondering if they think like me.
I ask a starfish for advice,
It just stares—how very nice!

Dolphins giggle at my plight,
As I ponder day and night.
"Is it bubbles or a thrill?"
Where's that answer? I need skill!

But oh, the fun that I have found,
In the ebb and flow around.
I'll keep jumping 'til I see,
The meaning's just to surf the spree!

Sifting Through the Sands of Time

With my shovel in the sand,
I dig for wisdom, isn't it grand?
A seashell whispers, "Take a break,"
While the sun stares down, quite awake.

Grains of wisdom slip away,
I just wish they'd like to stay.
A hermit crab steals my hat,
And I laugh—imagine that!

Each grain tells a tale or two,
About space and time, not much to do.
A seagull squawks, "You're a fool,"
But my shovel's still my tool!

The tide rolls in, it's time to go,
With a wink, I'm feeling slow.
Perhaps it's buried deep inside,
Where laughs and questions always hide.

The Lingering Quest

I roam the aisles of life's big store,
On the hunt for what's behind the door.
Neon signs flash "Find it here!"
But wait, is that just cheap beer?

Each shelf a riddle, each deal a tease,
I pick up a cactus, no thank you, please.
The map I follow is all a blur,
Leading me to a purple fur!

Do I need a guide, a potion or spell?
Or just a hot dog to know it well?
As I ponder with a hot cup of joe,
An owl hoots, "Just take it slow!"

But the fun's in endless displays,
Of thoughts and dreams in quirky ways.
So what if I wander, without a clue?
Life's a buffet—come, try it too!

Echoes of a Solitary Voyage

A boat adrift, it's just my crew,
A rubber duck and a fancy shoe.
Together we sail, no map in sight,
With a compass that points to the next bite.

I shout to the waves, "What's life's great plan?"
The fish reply with a hearty ban.
The seaweed giggles, the clouds roll by,
I wave to a passing bird in the sky.

Each ripple of water, a laugh, a sigh,
Sailing along, I give it a try.
A treasure chest filled with sweet dreams,
Oh, how life isn't what it seems!

So I dance on deck, with joy in my heart,
Finding snippets of wisdom, bit by bit, part by part.
In this quirky boat, I'll sail and glide,
For laughter and questions are my joyride!

Murmurs of Forgotten Paths

In the woods where leaves do dance,
I stumbled on an offbeat chance.
A squirrel mocked my every turn,
While I was lost, it took a burn.

Maps are scattered, so is my brain,
I asked a rock, but it felt lame.
Trees chuckled, giving secret hints,
But I just tripped on old man's prints.

With breadcrumbs trailing like my hope,
I ponder life, like it's a trope.
A bird swoops down with a cheeky grin,
Says, "Give it up! Start fresh again!"

I dance with shadows, laugh with light,
Maybe I'll find it… tonight, alright?
Reality's a joke we tell,
Where every wrong turn rings a bell.

Among the Stars of Possibility

In the sky where wishes float,
I asked a star, it just said, "Nope!"
A comet zooms, with a cheeky wink,
I laugh so hard, I can't even think.

Asteroids pass, they wave hello,
While aliens giggle below,
I scribble dreams on cosmic dust,
Hoping space won't bust my trust.

Gravity pulls, but so does fate,
I'm just a ball in this cosmic state.
Slipping through dimensions, what a ride,
Who knew the universe liked to hide?

Planets join in a silly dance,
Laughter echoes in cosmic chance.
I'll keep floating with this bliss,
Finding meaning in cosmic miss.

The Breath Between Moments

In the pause where chaos strands,
I find lost socks and rubber bands.
Taking a breath, I see it clear,
Life's meaning is just in the cheer.

Moments blend like paint on walls,
I juggle thoughts like bouncing balls.
Tick-tock clocks make silly noises,
While I'm left with all my choices.

Each heartbeat sings its quirky song,
Announcing I've been here too long.
Yet in that stretch between the beats,
Life serves its sweetest, strangest treats.

In the quiet where all meets,
I dance alone, feel life's beats.
With giggles echoing in time,
I draft my version, light and rhyme.

Whispers of the Unseen Journey

Feet shuffling down a winding road,
I met a frog with quite the code.
"Leap with joy!" he croaked with glee,
I laughed so hard, it set me free.

Through fields of daisies, dreams are spun,
Each flower tells me how to have fun.
Chasing tails of whimsical views,
Life's a game of happy clues.

Signposts point, but go astray,
A cow advised me yesterday.
"Chill out, dear — just wade through muck,
You'll find the gold if you're in luck."

With whispers swirling, secrets swirl,
In this crazy, wondrous world.
I'll leap through laughter, grin wide,
Striding boldly, with joy as my guide.

Threads of Solitude and Connection

In a crowd, I stand alone,
Wearing socks that don't quite match.
I wave at birds and greet my phone,
Does that count as a good catch?

Scouring life for treasures rare,
The coffee's cold, my time is hot.
I find a hairpin, someone's flair,
I guess that's all I've really got.

The cat stares hard, she knows my plight,
As if to say, don't lose your mind.
In the fridge, the lettuce is bright,
But my thoughts are still hard to find.

I laugh aloud, the world is strange,
Jigsaw pieces that never fit.
In the dance of life, I'll just range,
And hope tomorrow's a good wit.

The Fiction of Forever

I penned a letter to my fate,
But it bounced back with a smile.
It wrote, "You're just a small dot, mate,
Life's plot twists take a while."

I asked the moon what's next in line,
It giggled, shining rather bright.
I thought, is this a cosmic sign?
But what's wrong with a pizza night?

The stars conspire with a wink,
They say, "Just chill; your fate's a game."
While I ponder over time to think,
I burn my toast, oh dear, not the same!

So here I sit, a jester true,
In the theater of the absurd.
With popcorn dreams that might come through,
I chuckle softly; it's all just words.

Musings of a Soul on Fire

I sparked a flame with dreams of gold,
But burnt my toast and lost my lunch.
My ideas, vibrant yet uncontrolled,
Turn to smoke, how's that for a punch?

Outside my window, the squirrels jest,
With acorns round for winter's chill.
I ponder deep; they seem the best,
I can't help but admire their will.

I chase the high, a dance of glee,
While juggling thoughts like flaming pins.
But just as joy becomes a spree,
A neighbor's dog ends up in bins.

So here I am, a fiery soul,
With singed edges and laughter loud.
I'll take a bow; I lose control,
But in this chaos, I'm so proud.

A Dialogue with the Cosmos

I called the stars, they chuckled low,
"What's your question, little guy?"
I asked for wisdom, where to go,
They answered, "Try the local pie!"

The galaxies spun in playful dance,
While I tripped on a shoelace.
"Should I take chance or leave it to chance?"
They winked and said, "Just embrace."

Planets whispered secrets nice,
But I missed them while I sipped tea.
Now I'm left to ponder thrice,
Maybe all that matters is glee.

So I'll chat with the moon anew,
And throw in a joke or two for fun.
In the cosmic realm, we might just brew,
A nonsense life under the sun.

Echoes of a Silent Yearning

A penguin in a tux, confused on a dance floor,
He wobbles and slips, what else could he ask for?
With a martini in flipper, he looks for a date,
But the disco ball sparkles—oh, is this my fate?

Each fish in the sea, with secrets to share,
Gossiping about, who's got the best flair.
I question a crab, with his pinch and his stance,
"Have you found the answers, to give life a chance?"

The stars above giggle, they burst at the seams,
But float like balloons, lost in silly dreams.
Oh universe, listen, I'm ready to know,
Is life just a joke, or a circus to show?

In a world made of jelly, I stand with my spoon,
Chasing my thoughts, like a wild cartoon.
So if you hear whispers, of laughter and cheer,
Just call out my name, I'll still be right here!

Beneath the Surface of Tomorrow

A goldfish named Larry, with wisdom profound,
Wonders if wisdom is lost and not found.
He swims in circles, chin up, looking bold,
As the neighbor kids laugh, never do what they're told.

The clouds up above, are they pillows for dreams?
Or just floating fluff, bursting at the seams?
I ask a wise owl, perched high on a limb,
"Is this life all a game, or a whimsical whim?"

The sun plays peek-a-boo, hiding behind trees,
"Can life have a purpose?" I ponder with ease.
But the squirrels just chuckle, chase acorns for fun,
Their laughter ignites, my heart like the sun.

In the shadows of twilight, a rabbit hops by,
"Hey buddy, what's cooking?" I wave with a sigh.
He twitches his nose, "Life's just one big show,
So wear your best costume, and see where you go!"

Dreams Like Driftwood

A piece of driftwood, with stories to tell,
Lies on the beach, oh how it fell.
With each wave that crashes, it grins ear to ear,
"I once was a tree, now I'm just here!"

The seagulls cackle, their beaks full of sand,
Hollering secrets, as if life's a band.
They dive and they soar, with purpose unbound,
While I gather shells, and wonder what's found.

A turtle named Ned, moves slow with great care,
"What's the rush?" he muses, "It's a leisurely affair."
He dances with seaweed, sways with a smile,
"Let the tides take you, it's all worth your while!"

The sunset ignites, painting skies with delight,
As the stars take their place, one twinkling bright.
So here's to the moments, both silly and grand,
Life's a quirky parade, waiting for a hand!

A Searchlight on the Shore of Being

At the beach there's a lighthouse, with a flickering beam,
Guiding lost ships, in a whimsical dream.
It shouts to the waves, "You can't drown my light!"
While jellyfish giggle, dancing all night.

A crab pulls a prank, on a lobster nearby,
He snaps with a snap, "Is this my life? Why?"
But laughter spills out, like bubbles in foam,
As they splash like they meant it, out there on their roam.

The sandcastles grow, like towers of fun,
Complete with a flag, waving yellow and run.
But the tide rolls in quickly, with mischief and cheer,
"Pack up your dreams, my darlings, it's here!"

As waves wear down castles, the moon starts to yawn,
Whispering secrets, before it's all gone.
So grab your pink seashell, and dance with the sun,
In this funny old life, let's never be done!

Chasing Shadows in the Twilight

In the dusk we roam and play,
With goalposts that keep moving away.
We chase the light, all feelings bright,
Yet stumble on shadows, what a sight!

Questions swirl like leaves in air,
With answers hiding everywhere.
We ask the stars, they giggle loud,
Their twinkling winks, a teasing crowd!

A map of whims drawn with a pen,
Leads to corners that twist and bend.
Ride bicycles of thought, just so,
Till we hit a bump and lose control!

Yet laughter echoes through the chase,
Each twist and turn, a funny face.
In twilight's glow, we halt and stare,
At shadows dancing without a care.

Labyrinths of the Heart's Inquiry

In the maze where love and humor meet,
We wander clueless, with two left feet.
The heart, a puzzle, pieces askew,
Grinning like fools, what else can we do?

Questions bob like fish on a line,
With hopes that bubble, bright and fine.
Yet the more we ask, the more we roam,
Like a dog chasing tails somewhere far from home.

Maps of longing, scribbled in haste,
Lead to surprises, but none we taste.
We giggle and sigh at every blind turn,
Learning life's lessons, sometimes too stern.

But is there joy in every stumble?
With each twist and turn, we still can tumble.
In the giggles we find hidden gold,
In laughter, love's mysteries unfold.

The Compass of Uncertainty

With compass spinning, day and night,
We search for truth, a valiant fight.
But north is south, and east turns west,
Is it a quest or an unwelcome jest?

We trail along the paths of doubt,
With every turn, our hearts shout out.
'Is there wisdom hidden in folly?'
But the map just laughs, 'You're not that jolly!'

Every step feels right, then wrong,
Yet we hum our funny little song.
Through thick and thin, we clasp our fears,
Regaling them softly with laughter and cheers.

A compass? Ha! What a silly tool!
Guiding us with the grace of a fool.
Yet in this ride, we find delight,
In the uncertainty, we dance through the night.

Threads of Curiosity Weave

With threads of thought, we stitch and sew,
Creating patterns in the glow.
A tapestry of questions unbound,
Where humor and wonder are always found.

Each strand a whim, a curious jest,
We weave life's cloth, though it's quite a mess.
With needles of laughter, sharp and quick,
Poking at fabric, a comical trick.

We tie the knots of hidden dreams,
Unraveling seams with silly screams.
In every loop, a story brews,
Of quirks and quips that life reviews.

So let's keep weaving, side by side,
In threads of laughter, we'll take our ride.
For in this work of art, we find,
The joy of living, humor intertwined.

Tapestry of Unanswered Prayers

I asked the stars for guidance so bright,
They winked and giggled, what a sight!
The moon just shrugged, a lazy dream,
While I scribbled questions on a chocolate cream.

The sun, it laughs, as I chase my tail,
With maps that hint at an ancient trail.
Coffee spills tell stories, I sip in vain,
And the cat just meows, embracing my pain.

A squirrel's wisdom from the tree above,
Offers advice wrapped in a syrupy glove.
I trip on riddles in joyful glee,
As life shows me things only squirrels can see.

With each twist of fate, I roll my eyes,
Life's absurdity wraps me in its guise.
Like a jester dancing in a court of jest,
I ponder my questions and grin at the quest.

The Dance of Doubt and Desire

A tango with worry on a crowded floor,
Desire's a partner I simply can't ignore.
They twirl through the night, round and round,
While I step on dreams, which land with a sound.

My heart skips beats like a record on pause,
Doubt taps its foot, with its own set of flaws.
And laughter erupts from the back of the room,
As I trip on the steps of impending doom.

The DJ's advice: just let it all go,
So I mix up my feelings in a wild show.
Life's a dance-off with rhythm and sneers,
And I juggle my hopes with a bag of weird fears.

But oh, what a spectacle, this crazy affair,
As I summon my strength to throw back my hair.
With joy and confusion, I take a deep breath,
And twirl on the dance floor, embracing my jest.

In the Labyrinth of Self

In a maze made of thoughts, I wander around,
With mirrors reflecting a self I've yet found.
Each corner I turn, I bump into me,
Fumbling for answers like cold cups of tea.

A signpost reads 'Take the left fork at goo,'
While a talking snail claims it's the right way to you.
Puzzles and riddles spill out of my head,
As I ponder the meaning of the toast I just fed.

Walls painted with colors of memories lost,
Faded and whispering hints at their cost.
I chase down a shadow that looks like a friend,
But it giggles away, leaving me in a bend.

The exit is near—or so I have heard—
Yet I'm stuck in this tangle, how absurd!
And with a shrug of my shoulders, I laugh at the strife,
For what's a good journey without a dash of life?

Heartbeats of a Restless Wanderer

With luggage of dreams and a map made of foam,
I set out to find where I truly belong.
Each heartbeat's a compass, the rhythm's my guide,
Yet I end up at places where lost socks reside.

The road sings sweet songs of elusive delight,
While pigeons squawk secrets of the plight.
"Try a new direction," the wind seems to say,
But I trip on my laces and tumble away.

With laughter like echoes, my journey unfolds,
As I chase after sunsets and foolish gold.
The stars point and chuckle, "What are you here for?"
And I answer with hiccups, "I'm not really sure!"

Yet my heart keeps on beating, a rhythm so wild,
As I embrace every hiccup, like a curious child.
With a wink to the cosmos, I dance through the night,
For the wanderer's spirit shines ever so bright.

The Alchemy of Life's Mysteries

In a pot, the dreams do simmer,
With a pinch of hope, I start to shimmer.
The recipe's lost, I can't recall,
Mixing giggles with the tears on the wall.

A dash of chaos, a twist of fate,
Stirring in laughter, it's never too late.
Best we don't measure, just splash it all,
For who needs a guide when you can sprawl?

The wise old sages, they twitch and grin,
As I ask if they've ever been thin.
Life ain't a puzzle, more like a game,
Those seeking grandeur, I can't quite name.

In this cauldron of wonder, I'll twirl and dance,
For the secret ingredient might just be chance.
It's a carnival ride, don't hold on tight,
With confetti of dreams that take flight.

Conversations with the Infinite

I once had tea with the great unknown,
His jokes were cosmic, I felt overgrown.
"Why ask for wisdom when you can jest?"
"What's the point of life? Just enjoy the quest!"

He served a brew, stardust and foam,
Sipped slowly, I felt quite at home.
"Life's like a riddle wrapped in a pun,
Chase laughter, my friend, that's the real fun!"

His beard was the cosmos, wild and free,
"I lost my compass, but found some glee.
Just wander about without any plan,
Wear socks on your hands, be your own fan!"

So I left with a chuckle, a wink, maybe two,
Life's just a circus, and I'm in the zoo.
The infinite smiled as I skipped away,
A joyous reminder that I'll be okay.

Pages from an Untold Story

Once found an old book, its cover all frayed,
Filled with tall tales that laughter displayed.
Each page I turned, the plot went askew,
A dragon who danced? Why not, my view!

In the margins were doodles, a laugh or a frown,
Commentary from me as I scribbled a crown.
"Who writes this nonsense where cats fly in hats?"
No reason to fret, I just fed them some rats!

In the midst of the chaos, a moral appeared,
"Embrace the absurd, let go of your fear!"
Chased by a penguin, I swung from the vine,
This untold story, a laugh divine.

With pen now in hand, my journey's in sight,
Each chapter a giggle, the world feels so bright.
I'll weave together the silly and sweet,
For life's a grand tale, let's make it a treat!

The Art of Questioning Silence

In the quiet of moments, I ponder aloud,
As echoes of crickets form a soft crowd.
"Why don't clouds giggle, or stars break a grin?"
In silence they smirk, let the questions begin!

I shouted to shadows, "Hey, what's your dime?"
They whispered in riddles, in rhythm and rhyme.
"Life's an old game, try flipping the board,
Find laughs in the quiet, let your heart be adored!"

To ponder or waffle on what's unnamed,
I danced with the silence, I wasn't ashamed.
"Why can't we tickle the time as it flies?"
With snickers and cheers, let the giggles rise!

So here's to the hush that makes room for quips,
A canvas for laughter, with colorful scripts.
In each pause, there's joy, in whispers, delight,
Life's grand performance, let's laugh through the night!

Windows to the Infinite

Peering through glass, I see clouds drift,
My dreams in a blender, oh what a gift!
Lost in the colors, a whimsical sight,
Why is the sky both day and night?

Pigeons are juggling, a cat on the prowl,
I throw up my hands, can't help but howl!
The universe giggles, I'm just a guest,
Calendars spin, but I'm never stressed!

Stars wear pajamas, they sparkle and yawn,
I sip cosmic coffee, is it dusk or dawn?
Those meteors whizz by on their race,
Who knew the void has such a good pace?

Windows wide open, I let in the fun,
Life's a game show, who's next in the run?
Each label I find, a riddle in disguise,
When will I learn? Oh dear, I have no prize!

The Puzzle of a Fractured Heart

I found a piece under my bed,
It's shaped like a donut, filled with dread,
Fractals of laughter, oh what a mess,
Just grab some icing; I must confess!

Love notes in the fridge, age like fine cheese,
I laugh as I search; oh, where's my keys?
Puzzle of feelings—missing some bits,
Guess I'll just order a pair of new fits!

A heart made of chocolate, melted away,
I ate half for breakfast; what else can I say?
Filling up holes with laughter and snacks,
Can't spell all the answers, that's why I relax!

Fractured yet perfect, my heart's not unwise,
It dances in circles, while I just surmise,
Through laughs and mishaps, I'll find my way,
To stitch up the moments—oh! Where's my bouquet?

Memories of Tomorrow's Search

Tomorrow's already yelling, 'I'm here!'
While memory giggles, holding my beer,
Worn-out maps showing roads that don't lead,
But hey, let's keep wandering, it's all that we need!

Fuzzy snapshots, the past likes to tease,
I tripped on my laughter, stumbled on these,
The future's a party, but what's this fuss?
Is my invite lost, or am I just a plus?

Time tiptoes softly, in clown shoes, so bright,
Holding balloons, it dances with delight,
I make silly wishes, toss coins in the air,
Who knew nostalgia would wear polka-dots everywhere?

My brain's on a carousel, spinning with flair,
Memories and tomorrows, swirls of fair hair,
Caught in a loop, but doing just fine,
When I tune into whimsy, I pick up the line!

Between Now and Never

Caught between seconds, I juggle my dreams,
Is life like a movie? Or just silly memes?
Time wears a mustache, and dances on toes,
While clocks throw confetti, no one really knows!

If 'now' were a cake, I'd spice it with cheer,
Baking up moments, they sprinkle with beer,
Never is cautious, it rolls with a grin,
While today takes selfies, with cheese and a spin!

I ask for directions, my GPS moans,
Between here and there, I'm cloaked in big cones,
Can we take a shortcut, or should I just wait?
Time laughs like a devil, "Oh, isn't it great?"

Between this and that, it's a dance of delight,
Life's a riddle wrapped in an echoed insight,
So let's twirl with chaos, and sip on our glee,
For 'never' can wait; it's too stiff for me!

The Silence Between Thoughts

In the quiet pause of mind's race,
I search for wisdom in empty space.
Is that a thought or just a snack?
Life's little questions, always lack.

Juggling ideas, one slips away,
Like socks lost in the dryer's ballet.
Why does wisdom wear a disguise?
Perhaps it's hidden in some fries.

The clock ticks loud in thought's cocoon,
Echoing questions like a cartoon.
If laughter's the answer, where's the punch?
I'll muse while munching my lunch.

A sigh escapes, a chuckle near,
Philosophers sip their amber beer.
As thoughts twirl in a whimsical dance,
I might just miss my next "big" chance.

Fragments of a Dreamer's Path

I wander trails of scattered dreams,
With shoes untied, or so it seems.
Each step I take, a riddle spun,
Like trying to catch a fleeing bun.

The stars above are on my side,
Though one just fell, I laughed and cried.
A whisper calls from a candy shop,
"Find your truths by taking a hop!"

With pie in hand, I search the cloud,
In search of answers, I feel so proud.
But flavors shift and melt away,
What's life without a good soufflé?

So I dance a jig, a waltz of chance,
Embrace the chaos, join the prance.
For every piece I fail to find,
I'll laugh at fate, and eat my rind.

In Search of a Flicker

A firefly glimmers, then it's gone,
Like meaning at the break of dawn.
I chase the light through fields of green,
Wearing my thoughts like a costume sheen.

Do moths have answers? They flap and flutter,
As I trip on clovers and make a sputter.
"Is this the way?" I ask a bee,
Who buzzes loudly, "You're not quite free."

I toss a nickel into the breeze,
In hopes that luck takes me with ease.
But coins roll down a rabbit's hole,
What's gained by searching? Who's the goal?

And as I ponder in absurd delight,
I hear the stars giggling at my plight.
If flickers are fleeting, let's dance and sing,
Perhaps in laughter, we find our king.

The Unfurling Map of the Soul

Unroll the parchment, map of me,
Where X marks spots of missed glee.
A compass spins, it's lost its mind,
Where truths are wrapped in bubble bind.

I traced the lines of paths once crossed,
In search of meaning, I got lost.
With coffee stains and crumbs of toast,
I charted areas where I'm the most.

A treasure chest of quirks and jests,
Life's puzzles hide behind its quests.
Drawing with crayons, colors appear,
Each line a laugh, each shade a cheer.

So here I stand with half a clue,
A giggle turns each worry anew.
When paths diverge, I lose control,
And find new maps for my crazy soul.

Dancing with the Unknown

Twirl with shadows, laugh with light,
Lost my keys, but what a sight!
Salsa with questions, cha-cha too,
Where's the map? I haven't a clue.

Waltzing blindfolded, oh what fun,
Tripped on thoughts; now I'm on the run!
Cups of coffee, slips and spills,
Life's a party; let's pay the bills.

Frolicking finds in forgotten space,
Every misstep is a new embrace.
Life's a jiggle, a jester's song,
Join the dance; you can't go wrong!

So let's groove in this cosmic jest,
No grand prize, but we'll be blessed.
What's the meaning? Who knows, my friend!
Just keep dancing, it's the latest trend!

The Wisdom of Unasked Questions

What's the secret behind a sneeze?
Is there wisdom in wedged peas?
Why do socks disappear from the wash?
Is it a thief or a laundry nosh?

What's the deal with birds and their tweets?
Do they know secrets we'd love as treats?
Why is a raven like a writing desk?
Ask away! Or be a curious mess.

Should we fear the great unknown?
Or chuckle at the chaos that's grown?
Why do we ponder and twist our fate?
Got room for dessert? Let's contemplate!

Questions gather like raindrops on leaves,
Laughing as the universe weaves.
With every ponder, we tickle the void,
In the silliness, we're all overjoyed!

An Odyssey of Hearts and Minds

Off we go on this quirky quest,
With mismatched socks, we'll never rest.
Do we have goals? Maybe just a snack!
With laughter in tow, there's nothing we lack.

Hearts like balloons, soaring high,
Minds like sponges, ready to try.
Sailing on thoughts, what a fine sail,
Each whim a gust, let's avoid the nail!

Maps are overrated, oh can't you see?
Just follow the chuckles, that's the key!
In every jest, there lies a spark,
An arcane dance in the silly dark.

We'll trip over dreams, chase our fears,
While sharing a laugh or two, or cheers!
In this zany journey, so sublime,
Let's lose our way, and find the rhyme!

The Canvas of Infinite Possibilities

With a brush, I splat, and colors fly,
Swirl my thoughts like pancakes in the sky.
What's the masterpiece? Who really knows?
Each stroke a giggle, the laughter flows.

Patterns and doodles blend with rays,
Creating mayhem in delightful ways.
A splash of reason, a hint of fun,
Why be serious when chaos has won?

Shapes tumble gently, like dreams in flight,
Curved and contorted, a comical sight.
Each layer adds tales that make you grin,
In this wild gallery, let's dive in!

So grab a hue, let your spirit roam,
In this whirlwind canvas, we'll find our home.
With brushes of laughter and colors ablaze,
Life is a painting, let's create a maze!

Reveries of an Inquiring Mind

I ponder bread and butter, why it's spread so wide,
Lost in thoughts of jellybeans and a magic ride.
Do socks have secrets? Do they hide in drawers?
Why do pots and pans dance when I open doors?

The cat is plotting world fame, or so I believe,
While I chase after wisdom, wrapped up in my sleeve.
Thoughts bubble like soda, they fizz and they pop,
Do dreams get hungry, and do they ever stop?

Questions like balloons float up to the sky,
Why doesn't my toaster fly, oh why, oh why?
I search for the answers beneath every stone,
But maybe it's fun to know I'm never alone.

So here's to the curious, the nutty and the wise,
With twinkling thoughts and giggles that rise.
Every answer I chase is a smile in disguise,
Exploring the nonsense, what a wondrous prize!

The Language of Longing

I heard the fridge whisper sweet nothings at night,
As I dream of tacos and pie just out of sight.
Does ice cream crave company, or feel all alone?
Why do I eat leftovers when they've turned to stone?

A sock once said to me, 'Don't take life so fast,'
But I tripped over wisdom, and I fell at last.
Does coffee sneak gossip, or is it just me?
Lost in the bubbles of deep mystery.

I ask the wise goldfish for secrets to seek,
But all they provide is a constant cheek sneak.
Are dandelions pondering their fluffy fate?
Or just watching me wonder if I'm ever late?

Let's own our confusion, let's praise every quirk,
Each question a dance in this silly old work.
The answers elusive, like kittens at play,
But laughter is surely the best kind of way!

Maps of the Inner Landscape

A map of my thoughts has a squirrel on the trail,
Pointing to peanut butter and a giant snail.
I ponder why rhymes might be sweeter than pie,
And do clouds ever giggle, or are they too shy?

I explored the terrain where old socks are found,
Where dreams float like balloons, lost without sound.
The hills are quite wobbly, the valleys quite deep,
Where questions dance round as I tumble and leap.

Each path is a riddle, a puzzle in jest,
Why do I fall asleep when I'm thinking my best?
Yet every misstep feels just like a game,
As I sketch my own map with a wink and a name.

Here's to the journey, the twists and the turns,
And all of the lessons that each moment earns.
From questions to laughter, the joy is in view,
As I navigate nonsense, with friends old and new!

Chronicles of a Wandering Spirit

Oh, the tales I could tell from the edge of my bed,
Of journeys to fridge realms where sandwiches fed.
I've wandered through kitchens, I've battled with crumbs,
While pondering life's meaning, the riddle still hums.

Did the cookie know it'd crumble just right?
Or was it the fate of an unsuspecting bite?
The chairs have opinions, they creak and they moan,
Each whisper a riddle, each sigh a new tone.

In the land of lost socks, there's a council at play,
Debating the reasons we fumble each day.
I look for the signs in the fridge's cold stare,
And wonder if cosmos have feelings to share.

So I'll tote my pen, chart my fanciful quest,
While the cat rolls its eyes, taking life as a jest.
The answers are tangled like hair in a breeze,
But isn't the fun what brings us to our knees?

www.ingramcontent.com/pod-product-compliance
Lightning Source LLC
Chambersburg PA
CBHW071836160426
43209CB00003B/324